President
George H. W. Bush –
A Short Biography

By Doug West, Ph.D.

Table of Contents

Preface

Welcome to the book, *President George H. W. Bush - A Short Biography*. This book is part of the 30 Minute Book Series and, as the name of the series implies, if you are an average reader this book will take around 30 minutes to read. Since this short book is not meant to be an all-encompassing biography of George H. W. Bush, you may want to know more about this man and his accomplishments. To help you with this, there are several good references at the end of this book. Thank you for purchasing this book. I hope you enjoy your time reading about former President Bush.

Doug West
March 2017

Introduction

In February 1991, when the Persian Gulf War ended after US missiles and fighter planes shattered Iraq, and ground forces defeated the enemy force within 100 hours, Americans rejoiced at the power of their weaponry, their quick victory, and the appropriateness of their cause. President George H. W. Bush received praise for his strong leadership, and amid the excitement surrounding the return of US soldiers, he proclaimed a new world order in which countries committed to moral leadership would contain invaders and terrorists around the world.

The decisive outcome of the Persian Gulf War indicated that peace would reign, and Bush would be reelected. His public approval rating had reached 90 percent, a level far higher than any other US president. However, little more than 18 months later, voters ousted Bush from the White House. Despite his unprecedented popularity from military and diplomatic triumphs, Bush was unable to withstand dissent at home from a weak economy, rising violence in inner cities, and continued deficit spending. His term as president is a notable example of what can happen to a president who pursues foreign policy while ignoring domestic issues.

Chapter 1 - Early Years

"I do not like broccoli. And I haven't liked it since I was a little kid and my mother made me eat it. And I'm President of the United States and I'm not going to eat any more broccoli." - George H. W. Bush

Like many presidents before him, George Herbert Walker Bush came from a family known for its wealth and leadership in the private and public realms. He was born on June 12, 1924, in Milton, Massachusetts, but grew up in Greenwich, Connecticut, a prosperous town near New York City. His father, Prescott Bush, was a successful businessman. Prescott was president of Brown Brothers Harriman & Co. investment bankers, and served on the board of Pan American Airways, the Columbia Broadcasting System, and Dresser Industries. He was closely associated with the Republican political leaders, and served as the Republican senator from Connecticut from 1952 to 1963. George's mother, Dorothy Walker Bush, was from a wealthy family in Missouri. As a child, George spent summers at Walker's Point, his family's 10-bedroom home on 10 acres of land that jutted into the Atlantic Ocean at Kennebunkport, Maine. As a young boy he was called "Poppy," a name he would grow to detest by the time he reached early adulthood.

George attended an exclusive private school in Greenwich, and in 1936 he enrolled at Phillips Academy, a well-respected all-boys prep school in Andover, Massachusetts. George was very involved in his school; he was president of his senior class and the Greek fraternities, a member of the basketball team, and captain of the baseball and soccer teams. Bush met his future wife, Barbara Pierce, as a student, during a Christmas dance at the Greenwich Country Club. After a whirlwind romance, they decided to marry.

The day Japan attacked the United States at Pearl Harbor, Bush vowed he would fight to defend his country, and joined the Navy after he graduated from Phillips Academy in June 1942. For reasons that are unclear, officials waived the two years of college required for flight training, and Bush became America's youngest Navy pilot.

On September 2, 1944, Bush's fighter plane was hit while he was on a mission to attack a Japanese radio installation in the Pacific island of Chichi Jima. As smoke filled the cabin, he managed to strike his target. He then fought to keep the plane in the air. At 1,000 feet, one of his two crewmen bailed out, but his parachute tangled and he was killed. Bush jumped free of the plane next, while the second crewman failed to escape. After plunging into the ocean, Bush swam to a lifeboat that had been jettisoned from the plane, and was rescued by a US submarine. For his valiant service, he was awarded the Distinguished

Flying Cross and three Air Medals before returning home in December 1944.

Figure - Pilot George Bush during World War II

On January 6, 1945, Bush married Barbara Pierce. The couple had six children over the course of their long marriage. That fall, Bush enrolled at Yale University and majored in economics. Similar to his experience at Phillips Academy, he excelled academically and athletically. George was the fourth generation of Bushes to attend Yale. Like his father, he became a member of the Skull and Bones, a select secret society. He played on the baseball team that reached the finals of the 1948 national championship, only to lose to the University of Southern California.

After Bush graduated from Yale in three years, his father found him a job at Dresser Industries, an oil company. In 1948, he began cleaning and painting machinery as a trainee for the firm in Odessa, Texas. A few months later the company assigned him to California, where he worked as a salesman. After that position, he was relocated to Midland, Texas. As an employee of Dresser Industries, Bush saw the oil business up close and learned the day-to-day details he would soon need in his own business.

George and Barbara Bush found they liked West Texas and the bustle of the oil business. In 1950, George raised $350,000 from friends and family to go into business for himself with John Overbey, an independent oil man. Together they created the Bush-Overby Oil Development Company. The company bought oil rights and lined up the financial backing required to drill the fields. Two years later, Bush-Overby merged with another company to form Zapata Petroleum. The company prospered, and by 1954 they owned 71 oil wells. Bush established the headquarters for another business, Zapata Offshore, in Houston, and moved to Houston from Midland in 1959.

Like all families, the Bushes weren't without their share of tragedy; in 1950 their baby daughter, Robin, contracted incurable leukemia. Robin's death in 1953 devastated the couple, and as often happens with the death of a child, their marriage began to suffer. George grew more distant and Barbara focused her attention on their two remaining children, seven-year old George W. and eight-month-old John Ellis Bush, nicknamed Jeb. By the end of the decade of the 1950s, the Bushes would add three more children to the family, Neil, Marvin, and Dorothy.

George Bush made his first million dollars when the Zapata partners amicably split the business in the late 1950s. Part of the company split became part of Pennzoil through a merger. Now well off, he turned his attention to politics.

Chapter 2 - Entrance into Politics

"I have opinions of my own, strong opinions, but I don't always agree with them." - George H. W. Bush

George Bush cut his political teeth in 1960, when he ran for Harris County Republican Chairman in Houston. He won, and for two years under his leadership, the party grew in a predominantly Democratic environment. In 1964 he ran for the US Senate, but after easily winning the Republican primary, he lost the general election to the incumbent liberal Democrat Ralph Yarborough. The Texas political landscape had turned more conservative leading up to the 1964 election, giving Bush hopes of winning. The administration of President Kennedy had divided the Democratic party, especially in Texas. Kennedy's assassination in late 1963 united the party behind the now president and native Texan, Lyndon Johnson, thus squelching Bush's chance of defeating Yarborough. Many Texans considered Bush an arrogant outsider, despite his having lived in Texas for 16 years. Hampered by his Eastern mannerisms, he adopted those of a Texan and started wearing cowboy boots and cowboy hats, and exhibited a more down-to-earth attitude.

Bush ran for the US House of Representatives in 1966 on a platform critical of President Lyndon Johnson's spending on social programs, but supportive of the Vietnam War. He defeated his colorless Democratic opponent, Frank Briscoe. In Washington, Bush proposed no significant legislation and took a moderately conservative stance on most issues. He backed reductions in government waste and wanted voluntary prayer in public schools. He pushed for a part of federal funds to be returned to the states, opposed school busing to achieve racial integration, and fought against the federal registration and licensing of guns. As the Vietnam War dragged on, Bush changed his views on the war and called for American withdrawal. Despite his vote on busing, he supported a civil rights bill and the Fair Housing Act of 1968. This infuriated some of his conservative backers, but he still won reelection that year.

Encouraged by Richard Nixon and other Republicans, Bush ran for the Senate a second time in 1970. He thought he would again be facing the liberal Ralph Yarborough in the contest, but Lloyd Bentsen defeated Yarborough in the Democratic primary. Bentsen started with an advantage over Bush because most Texans were registered Democrats. As a fellow conservative, Bentsen cut into Bush's support and won the general election. Bush wrote to friend that the loss in the election "sent me to the depths."

Chapter 3 - The National Stage

"We are a nation of communities...a brilliant diversity spread like stars, like a thousand points of light in a broad and peaceful sky." - George H. W. Bush

After Bush's defeat in the 1970 Senate race, President Nixon stepped in and appointed Bush US Representative to the United Nations. Bush was aware he had little experience with foreign affairs, so he crammed intensely and even made a trip out to the Johnson ranch to seek L.B.J.'s advice on foreign affairs. In that post, he defended the American preference for a "two-China policy," which meant representation for both Nationalist China and Communist China. His position was weakened in 1971, when the president shifted policy and agreed to a single seat for the communists.

In early 1973, Nixon tapped Bush to serve as chairman of the Republican National Committee (RNC). Bush welcomed the change as he had been frustrated when he realized the permanent representative at the UN had little influence on foreign policy, and he found it difficult to deal with Henry Kissinger. Friction developed between the two men when Nixon's advisers pressured Bush to defend the president in the rapidly worsening Watergate scandal. Bush refused, saying the RNC needed some independence. As the crisis grew more dire, and Nixon's position became indefensible, Bush wrote the president on August 7, 1974: "It is my considered judgment that you should now resign. . . I believe this view is held by most Republican leaders across the country." On August 8, more than two years after the Watergate break-in, President Nixon informed Vice President Gerald Ford that he was going to resign the next day. Ford took the oath of office the following day in the East Room of the White House and delivered a hurriedly written speech before the assembled crowd and a national television audience.

When Nixon resigned, Bush lobbied President Gerald Ford to appoint him Vice President, and he appeared on the chief executive's shortlist. In a memo written for Ford, White House aide Bryce Harlow listed Bush at the top. He stated: "Strongest across the board; greatest weakness—regarded as intellectually 'light' by many top leaders in the country." But Ford chose New York-er Nelson Rockefeller instead and allowed Bush to pick any other assignment he wanted. He chose to head the US Liaison Office in China. Once again Bush received the consolation prize; Ford offered him a major European Ambassadorship, but Bush request China instead. The time in China was just a rest stop for George and Barbara, a time to put the heated politics behind them. "Politics is always going to be a part of me," Bush said at the time he went to China.

Figure - President Gerald R. Ford meeting with CIA Director-designate George Bush in the Oval Office in 1975

Bush returned to Washington at the end of 1975 when President Ford appointed him Director of Central Intelligence (CIA). In January 1976, Bush took over an agency in crisis. He stepped in at a difficult period, as Senate investigations uncovered a range of illegal acts committed by the Central Intelligence Agency since its founding in the 1940s. Bush worked to restore morale at the CIA, and improved the technology available to the agency when he obtained $500 million from Congress. He used the funds to build two satellite reconnaissance systems and four ground stations to intercept overseas communications.

His time at the CIA was short-lived, as Bush resigned from his post after Democrat Jimmy Carter won the presidency in November 1976. Bush then returned to Texas and his business interests, though he continued searching for an opportunity to get back into politics. As Carter's popularity plummeted, Bush considered running for the White House himself, and in 1979 he formally announced his bid for the Republican nomination at the National Press Club in Washington, DC.

Chapter 4 - Vice President of the United States

"As his vice president for eight years, I learned more from Ronald Reagan than from anyone I encountered in all my years of public life." - George H. W. Bush

George Bush faced several daunting obstacles on his path to the presidency, among them his lack of name recognition; his weak record in winning elections; and the candidacy of Ronald Reagan, the former Governor of California, who was very popular with conservatives. Bush's longtime friend James Baker signed on to run his political action committee. To win, Baker suggested a strategy similar to what Jimmy Carter had used in 1976, which was to go door-to-door in Iowa and New Hampshire to establish a personal connection with as many people as possible. Bush surprised many by finishing first in the Iowa caucuses, but Reagan solidly beat him in the New Hampshire primary. Although Bush did not win the nomination, he became known for labeling Reagan's promise to lower taxes, increase defense spending, and reduce the budget deficit as "voodoo economics."

Despite the harsh rhetoric of the primary campaign, after Reagan won the nomination he picked Bush as his running mate. The Iranian hostage crisis had drug on for over a year during Jimmy Carter's last year as president, and his approval rating was dismal at best with the American people. The team of Ronald Reagan and George Bush won the election of 1980 by a landslide over the embattled incumbent President Carter. Over the next several years, Bush headed one task force to slow the influx of illegal drugs into the United States and another to minimize government waste through deregulation.

Less than three months into Reagan's term in office, a twenty-five-year-old drifter from Colorado, named John Hinkley, Jr., shot President Reagan. Hinkley was waiting outside the Washington Hilton Hotel when Reagan and his entourage emerged from the side door of the hotel. Hinkley managed to get off six shots before he was tackled by the Secret Service officers. One of the bullets ricocheted off the limousine and struck the president, puncturing a lung and stopping just an inch from Reagan's heart. Bush, who as vice president was next in the line of succession to the presidency, was in Fort Worth, Texas, at the time of the attempted assassination. Bush returned immediately to Washington, DC, and took up the role as acting president during Reagan's recovery. Bush has been credited with handling this crisis with great tact and nerves of steel.

Figure - Assassination attempt on President Reagan
outside Washington Hilton hotel

Bush served on the National Security Council (NSC), and
the job ensnared him in a scandal. In 1986 and 1987 it
was revealed that President Reagan had approved an NSC
plan to sell weapons to Iran in exchange for the country's help in getting Islamic militants to release American
hostages in Lebanon. In turn, Reagan's National Security
Advisor, John Poindexter, used proceeds from the arms
sales to illegally fund American-backed guerrilla forces
fighting a leftist government in Nicaragua. These actions

by the NSC not only broke the law, they also violated Reagan's promise to never deal with terrorists.

As Congress investigated and some on Capitol Hill talked about impeaching the president, Bush denied any direct knowledge of the Iran-Contra Affair. He claimed the plan was carried out by lower-level members of the NSC. "I wish it hadn't happened," he said. "I think everybody, to the degree there were mistakes, should share in the blame." In reality, Bush was being insincere, and when he said he was "out of the loop" on Iran-Contra, most Americans doubted him. Despite the scandal, he sought the presidency in 1988. Bush's contenders for the Republican nomination consisted of Senator Bob Dole; Representative Jack Kemp; former governor of Delaware, Pete Dupont; and the Christian televangelist, Pat Roberts.

To persuade Republicans to choose him, Bush abandoned his previous moderate positions and made promises conservatives would want to hear. Foremost, he swore he would oppose any new taxes. If any congressmen should try to force him to do otherwise, he said he would tell them: "Read my lips: no new taxes." Bush tied himself to Reagan's coattails, claiming he would continue to add jobs to the economy and lower inflation. Bush's experience, organizational skill, and a well-funded campaign were too much for the other candidates and he won the Republican nomination.

When Bush began his campaign against the Democratic nominee, Massachusetts Governor Michael Dukakis, polls showed Dukakis nearly 20 points ahead. Many voters still distrusted Bush's answers about the Iran-Contra Affair, and others thought he lacked Ronald Reagan's guts and called him a "wimp." To counter that impression and play on fears that Dukakis was too liberal, Bush unleashed a stinging negative campaign. His manager, Lee Atwater, who considered anything fair and nothing sacred in politics, took the low road.

Bush claimed that Dukakis was unpatriotic for opposing the Pledge of Allegiance in schools, which was an exaggeration of his actual stance on the issue. Bush's supporters portrayed Dukakis as soft on crime. Bush ran advertisements claiming that under the Massachusetts furlough system, a black convict, Willie Horton, had committed rape on a weekend release from prison. The Bush television ads showed a prison with black inmates exiting the facility through a revolving door. Elizabeth Drew of *The New Yorker* said, "Never had the appeal to racism been so blatant and raw."

Bush took a chance for a vice president running mate in the young senator from Indiana, Dan Quayle. Quayle was from a prominent family of newspaper publishers and had made a name for himself in political circles in 1980 when he defeated the liberal icon Birch Bayh for his senate seat. Though Quayle was not the VP candidate recommended by Bush's advisors, Bush liked what he saw in Quayle and took a chance on him. To much of America, Quayle appeared to have come out of nowhere onto the national political stage with Bush. After some initial growing pains, Quayle proved himself as a capable running mate for Bush.

To many Americans, both candidates had little appeal, and the voters continued their tendency to stay away from the polls. Conservative columnist George Will summed up the feelings of many Americans when he called the first debate between Bush and Dukakis a "national embarrassment." He said, "Michael Dukakis was marginally less embarrassing than George Bush was, if only because his canned thoughts were ladled out in understandable syntax." Bush's attacks and his promise to continue the Reagan program brought him victory. The Bush and Quayle ticket defeated Dukakis and his running mate, Lloyd Bentsen, in the Electoral College by 426 to 111. Bush became the first serving vice president to be elected president since Martin Van Buren in 1836.

Chapter 5 - President of the United States

"You cannot be President of the United States if you don't have faith. Remember Lincoln, going to his knees in times of trial in the Civil War and all that stuff." - George H. W. Bush

In his inaugural address, President Bush tried to soften the harsh political atmosphere when he called for the United States "to make kinder the face of the nation and gentler the face of the world." He criticized the material greed of the Reagan years and praised those volunteers who spent their time fighting for the good of mankind—the people and organizations that made up what he called a "thousand points of light."

Since the Democrats were in the majority in both the House and Senate, the new president called for bipartisanship to solve the nation's problems. The following is an excerpt form the inaugural address:

"We need a new engagement, too, between the Executive and the Congress. The challenges before us will be thrashed out with the House and the Senate. And we must bring the Federal budget into balance. And we must ensure that America stands before the world united, strong, at peace, and fiscally sound. But of course things may be difficult. We need to compromise; we've had dissension. We need harmony; we've had a chorus of discordant voices."

"For Congress, too, has changed in our time. There has grown a certain divisiveness. We have seen the hard looks and heard the statements in which not each other's ideas are challenged but each other's motives. And our great parties have too often been far apart and untrusting of each other. It's been this way since Vietnam. That war cleaves us still. But, friends, that war began in earnest a quarter of a century ago, and surely the statute of limitations has been reached. This is a fact: The final lesson of Vietnam is that no great nation can long afford to be sundered by a memory. A new breeze is blowing, and the old bipartisanship must be made new again."

George H. W. Bush entered the White House as the decades-long Cold War ended with the collapse of the Soviet Empire and the communist system in Eastern Europe. Mikhail Gorbachev, President of the Soviet Union, withdrew his country's last troops from Afghanistan soon after; he announced in June 1989 that Poland and Hungary were free to determine their own fates without Soviet interference. The Berlin Wall fell in October of 1990, which led to the reunification of East and West Germany. The front page headline of the October 3, 1990, *New York Times* read "TWO GERMANYS UNITED

AFTER 45 YEARS WITH JUBILATION AND A VOW OF PEACE." This point in history marked the return of a nation divided between the communist East and the democratic West Germany. The German flag was unfurled in front of the Reichstag building in Berlin at midnight to announce to the world the reunification of a nation that had been divided for nearly five decades.

Figure – Official White House Portrait of President Bush in 1989

By the end of 1989 the Russians had retreated to their own country, and the very survival of the Soviet Union was called into question. Many factors brought the fall of the Berlin Wall and the weakening of the Soviet Union: the effects of America's containment policy in the Cold War; discontent in Eastern Europe with Soviet domination; the excessive Soviet military spending that was draining the federal budget; widespread corruption in the communist system; and Gorbachev's commitment to reform. Gorbachev's new openness became known as *glasnost*. Bush reacted cautiously to the turmoil in Eastern Europe, neither exulting over the demise of Soviet power nor providing much aid to countries struggling to establish their independence. In 1991, the Communist party was outlawed in the Soviet Union and most of the republics that had once been the Soviet State joined a loose economic federation called the Commonwealth of Independent States. The international struggle known as the Cold War, which had dominated much of the world's attention since 1946, was at last over.

Critics said Bush was still looking at Europe through the distorted lens of the Cold War, and that he should have acted more firmly to support those governments emerging from Soviet rule. His supporters, however, said he moved at just the right speed, and that overt intervention might cause reactionaries in the Soviet Union to undo Gorbachev's reforms. Bush's National Security Advisor, Brent Scowcroft, stated: "Our policy has to be based on our own national interest, and we have an interest in the stability of the Soviet Union. The instability of the USSR would be a great threat to us."

While Eastern Europeans moved toward freedom, the Chinese endured oppression. In June 1989, communist leader Deng Xiaoping ordered troops to fire into a large crowd of pro-democracy demonstrators at Peking's Tiananmen Square. Hundreds, maybe thousands, died in the carnage. The world reacted in horror at the massacre, which was covered extensively by the press. Acting in protest, President Bush suspended military sales to China and halted high-level diplomatic exchanges. Bush's critics thought his response to the Chinese was halfhearted, but Bush was determined not to destroy the US relationship with the most populous country on the planet. Bush told his advisors, "We must walk our way through this." At the same time, he sent an advisor to meet secretly with Chinese officials and assure them that relations would not worsen, and he soon agreed to sell satellites to China. Many Americans believed he appeased the communist rulers, but he argued that the United States could best transform China into a more open society through expanded trade and better relations.

President Bush sent American troops into Panama in December 1989, after the country's strongman, Manuel Noriega, rigged elections and declared that a "state of war" existed with the United States. Once pro-America,

Noriega backed the Sandinistas and became wealthy as a drug trafficker. Operation "Just Cause," as Bush called it, resulted in the deaths of 24 American soldiers and numerous Panamanian civilians, but also in the capture of Noriega. Soon after, Noriega was extradited to Miami, Florida, and indicted for drug trafficking. In 1992 Noriega was convicted on numerous counts of drug smuggling and racketeering and was sent to prison.

In June 1990, Bush met with Mikhail Gorbachev, and they agreed to reduce long-range nuclear weapons by 30 percent and stockpiles of chemical weapons by 80 percent. Before the end of the year, the president formally announced that the Cold War had ended.

Chapter 6 - The Persian Gulf War

"A new breeze is blowing, and a world refreshed by freedom seems reborn; for in man's heart, if not in fact, the day of the dictator is over. The totalitarian era is passing, its old ideas blown away like leaves from an ancient, lifeless tree." - George H. W. Bush

The invasion of Kuwait by over one hundred thousand Iraqi troops and nearly two thousand tanks on August 2, 1990, eventually led to United States involvement in a protracted war in the Persian Gulf region. To avoid re-paying billions of dollars of loans received from Kuwait during the eight-year war between Iran and Iraq during 1980 to 1988, Iraqi dictator Saddam Hussein revived old territorial claims and attempted to annex Kuwait as his country's nineteenth province. Saddam Hussein was an oppressive dictator who had devastated Iraq since 1979. In addition to harshly repressing all dissent with the coun-try, Saddam had used chemical weapons against his own people and started a senseless war with Iran that cost the lives of hundreds of thousands on both sides. The small oil-rich nation of Kuwait was a key ally of the US in the region, with valuable ports on the Persian Gulf. Saddam grossly underestimated the response to the invasion of Kuwait by America and the coalition forces.

President Bush feared that Saddam might next invade Saudi Arabia, and this would put him in control of 40 percent of the world's oil supply. Bush set to work and organized an international coalition of forty-three nations, thirty of which sent military or medical units to liberate Kuwait, and he petitioned United Nations Security Council members. By November the UN had imposed economic sanctions and passed twelve separate resolutions demanding the withdrawal of the Iraqis. Bush initially sent 200,000 US troops as part of a multinational peacekeeping force to defend Saudi Arabia, called "Operation Desert Shield." On November 8, Bush increased the US expeditionary force to more than 500,000 to "ensure that the coalition has an adequate offensive military option." Groups from other allied countries brought the troop level to 675,000. UN Security Council Resolution 678 commanded Iraq to evacuate Kuwait by January 15, 1991, or else face military action.

While Saddam Hussein had envisioned this as an isolated regional quarrel, Hussein's actions provoked an unprecedented alliance that included the United States and most members of the North Atlantic Treaty Organization (NATO). In addition to NATO, Hussein faced opposition from Iraq's former military patron, the Soviet Union, and several Arab states, including Egypt and Syria. The Iraqi dictator must have found Washington's outraged reaction especially confusing in view of recent efforts by the administrations of Presidents Ronald Reagan and Bush to aid Iraq. Behind-the-scenes US arms transfers to Iraq were kept from Congress from 1982 to 1987, in violation of the law. Washington had provided intelligence data to Baghdad during the Iran-Iraq war. President Bush had thwarted congressional attempts to deny agricultural credits to Iraq because of their human rights abuses. The Bush administration had also looked the other way at secret and illegal bank loans that Iraq had used to purchase $5 billion in Western technology for its growing nuclear and chemical weapons programs. Just a week before the invasion, Ambassador April Glaspie informed Saddam Hussein that Washington had no "opinion on inter-Arab disputes such as your border dispute with Kuwait."

Without informing Congress or the American people, Bush and his advisers decided early in August to use military force to expel Saddam Hussein from Kuwait. "It must be done as massively and decisively as possible," advised General Colin Powell, chairman of the Joint Chiefs of Staff. "Choose your target, decide on your objective, and try to crush it." The president characterized the initial deployments as defensive, even after General Norman Schwarzkopf had begun to plan offensive operations. Bush did not announce to the American people the offensive buildup until after the November midterm elections. Meanwhile, the US goals had increased from defending Saudi Arabia, to liberating Kuwait, to crippling

Iraq's war economy, even to stopping Saddam Hussein from acquiring nuclear weapons. UN sanctions were effective and cut off 90 percent of Iraq's imports and 97 percent of its exports. In January 1991, Secretary of State James Baker met with Iraqi Foreign Minister Tariq Aziz, but Iraq refused to consider withdrawal from Kuwait. Iraq would withdraw from Kuwait only if the United States forced Israel to relinquish its occupied territories. Bush and Baker disallowed this linkage, as well as any Arab solution that allowed Iraq to retain parts of Kuwait. In Bush's mind, Iraq's aggression should gain no reward.

Bush claimed he had the constitutional authority to order US troops into combat under the UN resolution, but he reluctantly requested congressional authorization. The ensuing debate lasted four days. The Democratic Senator George Mitchell of Maine summed up the situation this way: "An unknown number of casualties and deaths; billions of dollars spent; a greatly disrupted oil supply and oil price increases; a war possibly widened to Israel, Turkey, or other allies; the possible long-term American occupation of Iraq; increased instability in the Persian Gulf region; long-lasting Arab enmity against the United States; a possible return to isolationism at home." Senator Robert Dole of Kansas opposed the critics, stating that Saddam Hussein "may think he's going to be rescued, maybe by Congress." On January 12, after Congress defeated a resolution to continue sanctions, a majority in both houses approved Bush's request to use force under UN backing. Nearly every Republican voted for war; two-thirds of House Democrats and forty-five of fifty-six Democratic senators cast negative votes. Those few Democratic senators voting for war provided the necessary margin of victory for the decision.

On January 15, 1991, the UN deadline passed with no response from Iraq. The next morning, President Bush addressed the nation from the Oval Office, "Five months ago, Saddam Hussein started this cruel war against Kuwait," he said. "Tonight the battle will be joined." On January 16, 1991, Operation Desert Storm began with a spectacular aerial bombardment of Iraq and Kuwait. The headline on the January 17, 1991 edition of the *New York Times* read, "US and Allies Open Air War on Iraq; Bomb Baghdad and Kuwait Targets; 'No Choice' But Force, Bush Declares." Much of the war was brought directly into the homes of America for five weeks of extensive television coverage via Cable News Network enabling viewers to watch "smart" bombs hitting Iraqi targets and US Patriot missiles intercepting Iraqi Scud missiles. President Bush and Secretary Baker, through diplomatic efforts, kept the coalition intact, persuading Israel not to retaliate after Iraqi Scud missile attacks on its territory and keeping Soviet Premier Mikhail Gorbachev advised as allied bombs devastated parts of Iraq and Kuwait. Though the air campaign made steady progress in destroying Iraqi military positions, Saddam would not leave Kuwait. The decision was clear: ground troops would be needed to liberate Kuwait.

On February 24, General Norman Schwarzkopf, or "Stormin' Norman," as he was called, sent hundreds of thousands of allied troops into Kuwait and eastern Iraq. Despite Saddam's warning that Americans would sustain thousands of casualties in the "mother of all battles," Iraq's army put up little resistance. By February 26, Iraqi forces had retreated from Kuwait, blowing up as many as 800 oil wells as they retreated. Allied aircraft flew hundreds of sorties against what became known as the "highway of death," from Kuwait City to Basra. After just 100 hours of fighting on the ground, Iraq accepted a UN-imposed ceasefire. Iraq's military casualties numbered more than 25,000 dead and 300,000 wounded, while US forces suffered only 148 battle deaths, 145 non-battle deaths, and 467 wounded. The coalition total was 240 dead and 776 wounded. An ecstatic President Bush proclaimed, "By God, we've kicked the Vietnam syndrome." President Bush's approval rating reached 89 percent, the highest level that any president had ever recorded to that point.

Figure – General Norman Schwarzkopf (right) talks with General Colin Powell, Chairman of the Joint Chiefs of Staff, during a press conference regarding the Gulf War.

The war was expensive, initially costing $1 million per day for the first three months, and this did not include the ongoing expense of keeping an encampment of 300,000 allied troops in Saudi Arabia, Iraq, and Kuwait. The total cost of the war was estimated to be $54 billion, of which $7.3 billion was paid by the United States, with another $11 billion from Germany and $13 billion from Japan, and the remaining $23 billion coming from Arab nations. For the first time in the twentieth century, the United States could not afford to finance its involvement in a war.

Despite calls to do so, Bush chose not to send US forces to Baghdad to capture Saddam Hussein, even though the Iraqi leader was public enemy number one. Attempts during the fighting to kill or capture Saddam had failed, and Bush was hoping that the Iraqi military or disgruntled associates in the Ba'ath party would oust the Iraqi leader.

When Kurds in northern Iraq and Shi'ites in the south rebelled against Saddam, the coalition provided little assistance. As General Colin Powell stated, "If you want to go in and stop the killing of Shi'ites, that's a mission I understand. But to what purpose? If the Shi'ites continue to rise up, do we then support them for the overthrow of Baghdad and the partition of the country?" Powell opposed "trying to sort out two thousand years of Mesopotamian history," and Bush was wary of becoming deeply involved in the Mideast quagmire. Saddam used his remaining military to crush the domestic rebellions, which sent streams of Kurdish refugees fleeing toward the Turkish border. Public pressure convinced President Bush to send thousands of US troops to northern Iraq, where the UN designated a security zone and set up temporary tent cities. Saddam's survival created a situation that Lawrence Freedman and Efraim Karsh have compared to "an exasperating endgame in chess, when the winning player never seems to trap the other's king even though the final result is inevitable."

Under a Security Council Resolution, Iraq had to accept the boundary with Kuwait, which was demarcated by an international commission, and accept the presence of UN peacekeepers on its borders. Iraq was also required to disclose all chemical, biological, and nuclear weapons including missiles, and cooperate in their destruction. What the allied bombs had missed, UN inspectors were able to locate. Saddam Hussein's scientists and engineers had built more than twenty nuclear facilities that were part of a large-scale Iraqi "Manhattan Project." Inspectors were able to uncover and destroy more than a hundred Scud missiles, seventy tons of nerve gas, and 400 tons of mustard gas. By the fall of 1992, the head of the UN inspection team believed they had destroyed any capability Iraq had for weapons of mass destruction.

The outcomes from the war included the restoration of Kuwait, lower oil prices, resumption of peace negotiations between Israel and the Arabs, and a temporary revival of credit of the United Nations. In addition, improved relations with Iran and Syria brought an end to Western hostage-taking in Beirut. Teams of firefighters extinguished the last of the blazing oil wells ignited by the retreating Iraqis in November 1991. The burning oil wells produced a suffocating smoke that had spread across an area twice the size of Alaska and caused long-term environmental damage. An estimated 200,000 civilians died, largely from disease and malnutrition. Millions of barrels of oil fouled the Persian Gulf, killing more than 30,000 sea birds. Back in America, an undetermined but large number of US veterans of the Persian Gulf War found themselves plagued with various medical conditions, referred to as "Gulf War Syndrome," brought on by exposure to various toxic gases and radioactive exposure from ammunition.

Figure - Hundreds of Kuwaiti oil wells were set on fire by retreating Iraqi forces, causing massive environmental and economic damage to Kuwait.

"I think Desert Storm lifted the morale of our country and healed some of the wounds of Vietnam. I'm sure of it," Bush said after the war. And he welcomed "an era in which the nations of the world, east and west, north and south, can prosper and live in harmony."

Chapter 7 – Presidential Election of 1992

"Losing is tough." - George H. W. Bush

After the Persian Gulf War, oil prices dropped and the economy slid into recession. Bush, in the spring of 1991, reluctantly agreed to the demands of congressional leaders to raise taxes. The tax increase broke Bush's campaign pledge of "Read my lips: no new taxes." The breaking of his campaign promise immediately put Bush at odds with his conservative base and led millions of Americans to distrust the president.

By 1992, the economy was clearly contracting and consumer confidence was at a record low. The unemployment rate rose to 7.8 percent. To try to jumpstart the economy, the Federal Reserve Board slashed interest rates, with little effect on the economy. Further exacerbating the slump were the cuts in military and aerospace spending. To stay profitable, many companies laid off their US workers and shifted the jobs to low-wage developing nations. "Staying competitive in world markets" became the slogan often repeated by business leaders as they laid off their American workers. Those workers lucky enough to keep their jobs often found themselves working longer hours and depending on income from a working spouse to maintain their standard of living. The economic slump proved to be temporary, but the recovery came too late to help Bush as his popularity plummeted, from the post Gulf War highs, to only 30 percent.

With the triumph of the Gulf War and Bush's rising popularity in 1991, many considered his chances for reelection the following year a foregone conclusion. But the continued sluggishness of the American economy eroded his support. He was attacked from within his own party over taxes and government spending, and at the 1992 Republican National Convention, outspoken conservatives moved the party's platform away from Bush's more moderate beliefs.

Bush hadn't been able to resolve his struggles with Congress, and his attacks on his Democratic opponent, Bill Clinton, didn't produce significant results. A polished speaker, Clinton had mastered the town meeting, a new type of presidential debate that allowed candidates to stroll freely around the stage instead of standing behind a lectern, and to take questions directly from the audience.

Bush's appeal to moderate conservatives was affected by the emergence of a third-party candidate, H. Ross Perot, an eccentric Texas billionaire. Perot often appeared on television presenting a homespun approach to problems and captured the attention of the American public as a true alternative to the slick professional politicians. Perot drew support for his stance on two key issues: He wanted a more aggressive approach to reduce the federal budget deficit; and, as an independent candidate, he claimed he could break through stalemates between the parties that were slowing down legislation in Washington.

Bush continued to tinker with the sagging American economy and, as it worsened, he offered no significant plans to reverse its decline. In the 1992 campaign, he relied on his low-road tactics from four years prior and tried to portray his Democratic opponent, Bill Clinton, as unpatriotic for supposedly making a trip to Moscow while he was a college student at Oxford, and as unreliable for having lied about avoiding the draft during the Vietnam War. But the attack failed, and every time Bush alluded to Clinton's character, he exposed himself to questions about the Iran-Contra Affair. By 1992, new evidence from former Defense Secretary Caspar Weinberger's notes, Israeli intelligence reports, and other sources showed that Bush had lied about the scandal, and that he had approved the exchange of arms for hostages. It turned out that he was involved in important decisions about the Iran-Contra affair.

Americans criticized Bush for refusing to use military force in the Balkans against Bosnian Serbs who had launched a war of "ethnic cleansing" against Bosnian Muslims. Bush considered that battle a quagmire and not directly important to American security. In any event, the conflict had little influence on the presidential race. As Clinton's campaign manager said when asked to define the election's central issue: "It's the economy, stupid." With unemployment rising above seven percent, Americans were unhappy and, on top of that, the man who had said, "Read my lips: no new taxes," had approved a deal with Congress that raised taxes.

Despite President Bush's many foreign policy successes, he still lost his bid for reelection. The conservative *National Review* called him "an other-directed man in a pretentious 10-gallon hat," "a leader who lacked vision," and "a Connecticut Yankee in the court of King Ronnie." The Democratic Clinton/Gore team led in the polls throughout the campaign, and on election night, Clinton received the most votes, with a total of 43.7 million; Bush came in second with 38.1 million votes; and the independent Perot receive a substantial 19.2 million votes. In a three-way race, Bush finished with the lowest-percentage popular vote for an incumbent president since William Howard Taft. In addition, where Ronald Reagan had won 91 percent of the Republican vote in 1984, Bush won just 73 percent.

Figure – Former President George Bush and President Bill Clinton shake hands just after the 1993 inaugural ceremonies at the US Capitol.

As a result of the civil war in the African nation of Somalia, thousands of citizens were displaced and food supplies were greatly reduced, creating a famine in the country. As a lame-duck president, in December 1992 Bush sent 28,000 troops to Somalia to protect supplies shipped there for famine relief, and to prevent armed groups from terrorizing humanitarian workers. By the end of 1993, the US started to pull troops out of Somalia.

As is typical for outgoing presidents, on Christmas Eve, he pardoned six officials indicted for their roles in the

Iran-Contra Affair, most notably Caspar Weinberger. The president called his action compassionate and insisted, "Nobody is above the law. I believe when people break the law, that's a bad thing." Others saw his pardons as preventing trials that would reveal the truth—including the truth about him.

Chapter 8 - Post-Presidency

"Never ask anyone over 70 how they feel.
They'll tell you."
- George H. W. Bush

After Bill Clinton's inauguration as president, George and Barbara Bush flew to Houston where they planned on building a home. George Bush made it clear he wanted to retire quietly from the public eye, much like President Reagan had done. Bush told Bill Clinton after the election defeat, "Bill, I want to tell you something. When I leave here, you're going to have no trouble from me." Bush had grown weary of politics and was feeling the sting of defeat from the loss of the presidency.

In April 1993, George and Barbara did accept an offer to return to the Middle East and were given a royal tour of Kuwait. The trip to Kuwait City was to commemorate the Allied victory against Iraq in the Persian Gulf War, and the former president was using the occasion to raise a significant amount of money for the new Bush presidential library. Barbara would recall of the trip in her diary, "We drove to Bayan Palace and all along the way were people cheering and waving George Bush posters and American flags and Kuwaiti flags." The Kuwaitis gave George Bush their highest award during the visit.

Unknown to former President Bush and the Secret Service, there had been an assassination attempt planned for Bush's visit to Kuwait. Just days before the American delegation's arrival on April 14, the local authorities had foiled an Iraqi plot to kill the former president. The Kuwaitis arrested a total of seventeen people; many confessed to the assassination plot. The plan was to detonate a car bomb. The Kuwaitis found a Toyota Land Cruiser loaded with over a hundred pounds of plastic explosives. Once the Bushes and their entourage returned to America, the Kuwaitis informed US authorities of the plot. In response, the US sent experts to Kuwait to examine the device and interview the captives. The CIA bomb experts compared the detonator and the remote-control trigger to known Iraqi explosives, and they were a match. After additional information was gathered by the FBI, the Clinton administration concluded the Iraqi leader Saddam Hussein was behind the attempt on former President Bush. In retaliation, President Clinton ordered a cruise missile strike on the headquarters of the Iraqi Intelligence Service on June 25, 1993. This was the first time a foreign power had attempted an assassination of a sitting or former president of the United States.

Bush provided helpful advice to his son, George W. Bush, when he ran for president in 2000. The elder Bush served as an unofficial advisor to George W. after he entered the White House. Reports circulated that father and son disagreed over the invasion of Iraq, with the elder Bush more dubious about launching the attack. The senior Bush remained a steady, vocal, and sometimes emotional defender of his son throughout his presidency.

In January 2005, President George W. Bush enlisted the help of his father and former president, Bill Clinton, to raise money for the victims of a tsunami that struck the nations around the Indian Ocean. Later that year, the two men joined forces to raise funds for relief efforts following Hurricane Katrina, which had devastated much of the Gulf Coast in the fall. The Bush-Clinton Katrina Fund raised over $130 million to provide relief from the damage of the hurricane in Alabama, Louisiana, and Mississippi.

Figure - Former President George H. W. Bush and First Lady Barbara Bush react during remarks by President George W. Bush during the Christening Ceremony for the aircraft carrier USS George H. W. Bush in Newport News, Virginia, Saturday, October 7, 2006.

Although Bush largely avoided active participation in public affairs beyond his disaster relief efforts and lucrative public speaking engagements, he did receive a great deal of media attention with several parachute jumps to mark important events in his life. Bush celebrated his 75th and 80th birthdays by skydiving; and in 2007, at the age of 83, he jumped safely to the ground to commemorate the completion of renovations made to the George Bush Presidential Library and Museum at Texas A&M University.

George Bush has had his share of health scares in his elder years. In 2012, he spent Christmas in intensive care for a bronchitis-related cough and other medical issues. The former president was hospitalized in 2015 after falling at his Maine summer home and breaking a bone in his neck.

In January of 2017, both George and Barbara Bush were admitted to the hospital. George was admitted January 15, after he experienced shortness of breath. He was later admitted to the Intensive Care Unit to address an acute respiratory problem stemming from pneumonia, according to a statement from the Bush family. The former first lady was admitted a few days later to the same hospital as a precaution because she was experiencing fatigue and coughing. Both George and Barbara were released by the end of January. According to the family spokesman, Jim McGrath, "He is thankful for the many prayers and kind messages he received during his stay, as well as the world-class care that both his doctors and nurses provided."

Through the January 2017 hospital stay forced both Bushes to miss the inauguration of Donald Trump as president, the couple was able to attend the Superbowl LI football game and assist with the opening coin toss. The former president, age 92, wore a suit without a tie, while his wife of 71 years donned a blue blouse, red scarf, and beige slacks to kick off the match between the Atlanta Falcons and the New England Patriots in Houston, Texas. The former president was taken to the coin toss in a wheelchair while his wife rode alongside him in a golf cart.

The End

Thank you for reading my book. I hope you found it worth your time and money. Please don't forget to leave a review for this short book. I read each review and they help me become a better writer.

- Doug

George H.W. Bush Timeline

June 12, 1924 - George H. W. Bush is born in Milton, Massachusetts, to Dorothy Walker Bush and George Herbert Walker Bush. He is the second of five children.

1937-1942 - George Bush, known as "Poppy," attends Phillips Academy in Andover, Massachusetts. In 1940 he contracts a staph infection that puts him in the hospital. He repeats a year at Andover.

December 7, 1941 - The Japanese attack Pearl Harbor. Bush hears news of the attack while walking across campus. A few weeks later at a Christmas dance, he meets Barbara Pierce.

June 12, 1942 - Bush enlists in the Navy on his 18th birthday, which also happens to be the day he graduates from Andover. On June 9, 1943, he becomes the youngest commissioned pilot in the naval air service when he is presented with ensign bars and gold wings.

September 2, 1944 - Bush is shot down over a Japanese island, Chichi Jima. Bush bails and is rescued by the submarine USS Finback and spends a month on the sub before being dropped off in Midway to return to his squadron aboard the San Jacinto.

January 6, 1945 - George H. W. Bush marries Barbara Pierce while on leave in 1945. The war ends before he returns to duty, and he is honorably discharged on September 18, 1945.

July 6, 1946 - George and Barbara's first son, George Walker Bush, is born in New Haven, Connecticut, while Bush is a student at Yale. Bush graduates in two and a half years with honors, is captain of the baseball team, and is admitted to the elite secret society, Skull and Bones.

Summer 1948 - Upon graduating from Yale, Bush takes a job in the oil industry with Dresser Industries and moves his family to West Texas.

December 20, 1949 - George and Barbara's second child, Pauline Robinson Bush, who will be called Robin, is born in Compton, California, where Bush's job has taken the family.

1952 - Bush co-founds Zapata Petroleum.

February 11, 1953 - John Ellis Bush is born. Known as "Jeb," his name is derived from his initials. A few weeks after Jeb is born, his three-year-old sister Robin is diagnosed with leukemia.

October 12, 1953 - George and Barbara's daughter Robin dies of leukemia. The Bushes hold a small memorial ceremony in New York, where she received treatment, before returning to their young sons in Texas.

January 22, 1955 - Neil Mallon Bush, the Bushes' fourth child, is born in Midland, Texas.

October 22, 1956 - Marvin Pierce Bush, the Bushes' fifth child and youngest son, is born.

August 18, 1959 - Dorothy "Doro" Bush is born. Soon after her birth, the family moves to Houston.

1964 - Bush unsuccessfully runs against liberal Ralph Yarborough for the US Senate seat from Texas.

1966 - Bush wins a seat in the US Congress.

1970 - Bush gives up his congressional seat to again challenge Ralph Yarborough for the US Senate. Bush loses the election.

December 11, 1970 - Keeping a promise to find Bush a job if his bid for US Senate failed, Richard Nixon announces his appointment of Bush as US Ambassador to the United Nations.

January 1973 - Bush leaves the United Nations to become chairman of the Republican National Committee.

August 6, 1974 - In a cabinet meeting on August 6, 1974, Bush tells President Nixon that Watergate is sapping public confidence. The next day, he sends a letter to the president suggesting that he resign. President Nixon announces his resignation on August 8, 1974.

1974 - President Ford offers Bush an ambassadorship in the country of his choosing. Bush chooses China and becomes the US Liaison in Beijing (then Peking).

1975 - While in China, Bush receives a cable from President Ford and Secretary of State Henry Kissinger asking him to return to Washington to become the Director of Central Intelligence.

May 1, 1979 - Bush announces his candidacy for president.

January 21, 1980 - Bush wins a surprise victory over Republican front-runner, California Governor Ronald Reagan, in the Iowa caucus.

May 26, 1980 - Bush officially pulls out of the race for the Republican nomination.

July 16, 1980 - At the Republican National Convention in Detroit, Bush receives a phone call in his hotel room from Ronald Reagan, asking him to be the vice-presidential nominee. Bush accepts the nomination and Reagan's platform.

November 4, 1980 - Reagan-Bush defeats Carter-Mondale by a wide margin.

January 20, 1981 - George Bush is sworn in as the nation's 41st vice president.

March 30, 1981 - President Reagan is shot outside the Washington, DC, Hilton Hotel. Vice President Bush's reaction to the assassination attempt, especially his restraint, demonstrated in even small gestures like not sitting in the president's chair in cabinet meetings, cements the relationship between Reagan and Bush.

December 3, 1986 - In his first public statement about the Iran-Contra affair, Vice President Bush admits that "mistakes were made."

October 13, 1987 - George Bush announces his presidential candidacy for the second time.

August 18, 1988 - Bush accepts the Republican nomination at the convention in New Orleans.

November 8, 1988 - Bush-Quayle defeats Dukakis-Bentsen, capturing 40 states and 53 percent of the popular vote.

January 20, 1989 - George H. W. Bush is inaugurated as the 41st President of the United States.

June 3, 1989 - The Chinese government brutally suppresses an uprising in Tiananmen Square. Bush's reaction is criticized for not being tough enough.

November 9, 1989 - The Berlin Wall falls. Bush famously says he will not dance on the wall and is concerned that celebrations of victory by the American president will provoke a backlash in the Soviet Union.

December 20, 1989 - In response to the murder of a US Navy seaman and the beating of two American witnesses by members of the Panamanian Defense Force, the United States invades Panama and captures Panamanian dictator Manuel Noriega to bring him to trial on drug trafficking charges in the United States.

June 26, 1990 - Bush breaks his "no new taxes" pledge when he agrees to put taxes on the table in negotiating a budget deal with congressional Democrats.

August 2, 1990 - Iraqi dictator Saddam Hussein invades neighboring Kuwait in a dispute over oil fields.

September 30, 1990 - Bush and the bipartisan budget committee announce their budget agreement in a Rose

Garden ceremony. Many in the Republican party reject the plan for the increase in taxes.

November 15, 1990 - Bush signs the Clean Air Act Amendments of 1990. *The New York Times* refers to the passage of the Clean Air Act Amendments of 1990 as the single most distinguished policy achievement of the Bush administration.

January 16, 1991 - Operation Desert Storm begins. The first phase of the war is an air assault. The ground offensive begins five weeks later and will last only 100 hours before the decision is made to end the war.

February 28, 1991 - A ceasefire is declared in the Persian Gulf War. On March 3, Iraqi and coalition military leaders meet to dictate the terms.

July 1, 1991 - Bush nominates Clarence Thomas to the Supreme Court to fill the seat vacated by Thurgood Marshall. The nomination comes under criticism when a former employee of Thomas, Anita Hill, alleges that he sexually harassed her.

February 1992 - President Bush announces his candidacy for re-election. Pat Buchanan, a speechwriter for former Republican presidents, challenges Bush in the primaries.

April, 29, 1992 - Riots break out in Los Angeles after four policemen caught on videotape beating a black man, Rodney King, are acquitted of the charges. Bush is criticized for his slow and, to many, inadequate reaction.

October 1, 1992 - Wealthy businessman Ross Perot re-enters the presidential race as a third-party candidate. After declaring his candidacy in February, Perot had dropped out in July, but rejoins the race in October.

November 4, 1992 - Democratic candidate William J. Clinton defeats Bush and becomes the 42nd President of the United States.

January 20, 2001 - Bush attends the inauguration of his son, George W. Bush, as the 43rd President of the United States. It is the first time a father and son have both been elected president since John and John Quincy Adams almost 200 years before.

October 7, 2006 - Former President George H. W. Bush and First Lady Barbara Bush attend a christening ceremony for the aircraft carrier USS George H. W. Bush in Newport News, Virginia.

January 2017 – Both George and Barbara Bush are hospitalized for various medical conditions.

Acknowledgements

I would like to thank Lisa Zahn for her help in preparation of this book. The quotes are from brainyquote.com. All the photographs are from the public domain.

References and Further Reading

Bush, G. W. 41 *A Portrait of My Father*. Crown Publishers. 2014.

Hamilton, N.A. and I.C. Friedman. *Presidents – A Biographical Dictionary*. Third Edition. Checkmark Books. 2010.

Naftali, T. *George H. W. Bush*. Time Books. 2007.

Reeves, T. C. *Twentieth-Century America: A Brief History*. Oxford University Press. 2000.

West, D. *President Ronald Reagan – A Short Biography*. C&D Publications. 2017.

Bakkila, B. Former President George H. W. Bush and Barbara Get Massive Applause at Super Bowl After Hospitalization. February 5, 2017 http://people.com/politics/super-bowl-2017-george-hw-bush-coin-toss/ Accessed February 17, 2017.

George H. W. Bush released from hospital. January 30, 2017. *USA Today*. http://www.usatoday.com/story/news/politics/2017/01/30/george-hw-bush-released-hospital/97251354/ Accessed February 17, 2017.

Timeline: George H. W. Bush's Life. PBS. http://www.pbs.org/wgbh/americanexperience/features/timeline/bush/ Accessed March 10, 2017.

About the Author

Doug West is a retired engineer, small business owner, and experienced non-fiction writer with several books to his credit. His writing interests are general, with expertise in science, history, biographies, numismatics, and "How-to" topics. Doug has a B.S. in Physics from the Missouri School of Science and Technology and a Ph.D. in General Engineering from Oklahoma State University. He lives with his wife and little dog, "Scrappy," near Kansas City, Missouri. Additional books by Doug West can be found at http://www.amazon.com/Doug-West/e/B00961PJ8M. Follow the author on Facebook at https://www.facebook.com/30minutebooks.

Figure – Doug West (photo by Karina Cinnante-West)

Additional Books by Doug West

Buying and Selling Silver Bullion Like a Pro

How to Write, Publish, and Market Your Own Audio Book

A Short Biography of the Scientist Sir Isaac Newton

A Short Biography of the Astronomer Edwin Hubble

Galileo Galilei – A Short Biography

Benjamin Franklin – A Short Biography

The American Revolutionary War – A Short History

Coinage of the United States – A Short History

John Adams – A Short Biography

In the Footsteps of Columbus (Annotated) Introduction and Biography Included (with Annie J. Cannon)

Alexander Hamilton – Illustrated and Annotated (with Charles A. Conant)

Harlow Shapley – Biography of an Astronomer

Alexander Hamilton – A Short Biography

The Great Depression – A Short History

Jesse Owens, Adolf Hitler and the 1936 Summer Olympics

Thomas Jefferson – A Short Biography

Gold of My Father – A Short Tale of Adventure

Making Your Money Grow with Dividend Paying Stocks – Revised Edition

The French and Indian War – A Short History

The Mathematician John Forbes Nash Jr. – A Short Biography

The British Prime Minister Margaret Thatcher – A Short Biography

Vice President Mike Pence – A Short Biography

President Jimmy Carter – A Short Biography

President Ronald Reagan – A Short Biography

Index

F

Ford, Gerald 12

G

Gorbachev, Mikhail 22, 26, 31
Greenwich Country Club 4
Gulf War iii, 1, 27, 33, 36, 37, 38, 43, 55

H

Hinkley, John 16
Horton, Willie 19
Houston, Texas 7, 9, 43, 48, 51
Hurricane Katrina 45
Hussein, Saddam 27, 28, 29, 30, 31, 34, 35, 44, 54

I

Iowa 15, 52
Iran-Contra 18, 19, 39, 42, 53
Iranian hostage crisis 15
Iraq 1, 27, 28, 30, 31, 32, 33, 34, 35, 43, 45

J

John Ellis Bush 7, 50

K

Kennebunkport, Maine 3
Kissinger, Henry 11, 52
Kuwait 27, 28, 29, 31, 32, 33, 35, 36, 43, 44, 54

Made in the USA
Las Vegas, NV
11 February 2022

43744935R00046